Welcome to "In the Line of Faith: A 50-State Firefighter Devotional," a journey that transcends geographical boundaries to explore the profound spirituality within the firefighting community across America. This devotional is a heartfelt tribute to the courageous men and women who serve as the frontline guardians of their communities in all 50 states. As we embark on this spiritual odyssey, each page unveils the inspirational stories, reflections, and verses that encapsulate the indomitable spirit of these dedicated firefighters.

From the bustling cities to the serene landscapes, each state carries its unique essence, and within it, the flame of faith burns brightly. This devotional is more than a collection of words; it is a celebration of the shared commitment, resilience, and unwavering devotion that bind firefighters together in the line of duty. Join us as we delve into the heart of each state, discovering the timeless principles that guide these heroes through challenges and triumphs. May these pages kindle a flame of inspiration in your own heart as we honor the brave souls who stand "In the Line of Faith."

Week 1 - Dedication of Volunteer Firefighters

Verse of the Week: "Whatever you do, work at it with all your heart, as working for the Lord, not for human masters." - Colossians 3:23 (NIV)

Introduction: This week, our devotional journey focuses on the dedication of volunteer firefighters, the unsung heroes who selflessly serve their communities. Join us as we explore the theme of dedication, drawing inspiration from these individuals who exemplify a commitment to the well-being and safety of others.

Devotional: Volunteer firefighters, embodying the spirit of selflessness, dedicate their time, skills, and hearts to protect and serve their communities. Whether responding to emergencies, participating in training, or offering support to those in need, these heroes showcase a commitment that goes beyond duty—it is a calling rooted in love for their neighbors. Their dedication mirrors the biblical encouragement to work with all one's heart, as if working for the Lord. As we reflect on the commitment of volunteer firefighters, may we be inspired to approach our own endeavors with a similar dedication, recognizing the impact of wholehearted service.

Reflection: Consider moments in your life when you witnessed or experienced the dedication of others. Reflect on the impact of wholehearted service and commitment.

Prayer: Gracious God, we thank you for the dedication of volunteer firefighters. Bless them with strength, resilience, and a sense of purpose in their service. May their example inspire us to approach our own responsibilities with a wholehearted commitment, recognizing the value of selfless service to others. Amen.

Action: In the spirit of dedication, identify an area in your life where you can give wholehearted service. Whether it's within your family, community, or workplace, approach your responsibilities with commitment and love, knowing that your efforts make a meaningful impact.

Week 2 - "Courage in California"

Verse of the Week: "Be strong and courageous. Do not be afraid; do not be discouraged, for the Lord your God will be with you wherever you go." - Joshua 1:9 (NIV)

Introduction: As we embark on our devotional journey through the states, we begin in the golden state of California. This week, we focus on the theme of courage, inspired by the fearless firefighters who battle blazes across the diverse landscapes of California. Join us in exploring the courage that emanates from the heart of the Golden State.

Devotional: Amidst the breathtaking landscapes of California, we find stories of courageous firefighters who, in the face of raging wildfires, embody a profound bravery that goes beyond the call of duty. Their unwavering commitment to protecting communities and facing the formidable forces of nature is a testament to the resilience that courage can ignite. As we reflect on the challenges they confront, may their spirit kindle a flame within us – a flame that empowers us to confront our own trials with a bold and unyielding resolve.

Reflection: Consider the ways in which courage has manifested in your life this week. Reflect on the challenges you faced and the strength that emerged from within.

Prayer: Heavenly Father, we thank you for the courage exhibited by the firefighters in California. Grant us the strength to face our challenges with bravery and resilience. May your guiding light lead us through every trial. Amen.

Action: Inspired by the courage of California's firefighters, take a practical step to confront a fear or challenge in your own life. Whether big or small, may this action be a testament to your growing courage.

Week 3 - "Strength in Texas"

Verse of the Week: "The Lord is my strength and my shield; my heart trusts in him, and he helps me. My heart leaps for joy, and with my song I praise him." - Psalm 28:7 (NIV)

Introduction: This week, our devotional journey takes us to the expansive landscapes of Texas, where the spirit of strength runs as deep as the Lone Star State itself. Drawing inspiration from the resilient firefighters who face challenges head-on, we explore the theme of strength and the fortitude that defines the Texan spirit.

Devotional: In the heart of Texas, amidst the vast plains and bustling cities, we find firefighters embodying a unique strength that mirrors the indomitable spirit of this great state. From battling wildfires to responding to emergencies, these heroes exhibit a strength that goes beyond physical prowess – it is a strength grounded in determination, courage, and a deep commitment to serving others. As we reflect on the challenges faced by Texas firefighters, may we draw inspiration to cultivate a similar inner strength within ourselves, allowing it to be our shield in times of adversity.

Reflection: Consider the sources of strength in your own life. Reflect on moments when you felt resilient, and recognize the inner fortitude that enables you to face challenges.

Prayer: Gracious God, we seek your strength as we navigate the challenges of life. Bless the firefighters in Texas with unwavering courage and resilience. May their example inspire us to find strength in you, knowing that with you as our shield, we can face any trial. Amen.

Action: In the spirit of Texan strength, engage in an act of physical or mental resilience this week. Whether it's a challenging workout or confronting a personal obstacle, let this action be a testament to the strength that resides within you.

Week 4 - "Hope in Florida"

Verse of the Week: "For I know the plans I have for you, declares the Lord, plans for welfare and not for evil, to give you a future and a hope." - Jeremiah 29:11 (ESV)

Introduction: This week, our devotional journey takes us to the sunshine state of Florida, where amidst the warm breezes and coastal beauty, firefighters embody hope in the face of adversity. Join us as we explore the theme of hope, drawing inspiration from the dedicated heroes who navigate challenges with optimism and determination.

Devotional: In the vibrant state of Florida, where the sun kisses the horizon, firefighters stand as beacons of hope. They bravely confront hurricanes, wildfires, and various emergencies, demonstrating a resilient optimism that inspires us all. Their commitment to protecting lives and property radiates a sense of hope that transcends circumstances. As we reflect on their endeavors, may we embrace the transformative power of hope in our own lives, finding strength in the belief that a brighter future awaits, even in the midst of challenges.

Reflection: Consider moments in your life when hope has played a significant role. Reflect on how hope has influenced your perspective and actions in challenging situations.

Prayer: Heavenly Father, we thank you for the hope exhibited by the firefighters in Florida. Bless them with unwavering optimism and strength. May their example inspire us to cultivate a hopeful spirit, trusting in your plans for a future filled with promise. Amen.

Action: In the spirit of hope, engage in an act of kindness or encouragement for someone facing challenges. Let this action be a reflection of the hope that you carry within, bringing positivity to those around you.

Week 5 - "Compassion in New York"

Verse of the Week: "And above all these put on love, which binds everything together in perfect harmony." - Colossians 3:14 (ESV)

Introduction: This week, our devotional journey takes us to the bustling and diverse state of New York, where amidst the cityscape and rolling hills, firefighters exemplify compassion in action. Join us as we explore the theme of compassion, drawing inspiration from the selfless acts of kindness demonstrated by these heroes in the Empire State.

Devotional: In the heart of New York, where the rhythm of city life meets the tranquility of nature, firefighters exhibit a profound compassion that transcends boundaries. From rescues in urban landscapes to aiding communities in times of need, their acts of kindness and selflessness create a harmonious tapestry of compassion. As we reflect on the compassion shown by New York's firefighters, may their example inspire us to embrace love as a binding force, fostering unity and harmony in our relationships and communities.

Reflection: Consider moments in your life when acts of compassion made a lasting impact. Reflect on how compassion has the power to bring people together and create harmony.

Prayer: Gracious God, we thank you for the compassion demonstrated by the firefighters in New York. Bless them with continued kindness and empathy. May their example inspire us to lead lives filled with love and compassion, harmonizing our interactions with others. Amen.

Action: In the spirit of compassion, extend a helping hand or offer support to someone in need this week. Let this action be a manifestation of the love and compassion that binds communities together.

Week 6 - "Resilience in Colorado"

Verse of the Week: "The Lord is my rock, my fortress, and my savior; my God is my rock, in whom I find protection. He is my shield, the power that saves me, and my place of safety." - Psalm 18:2 (NLT)

Introduction: This week, our devotional journey takes us to the picturesque landscapes of Colorado, where the majestic mountains and open plains set the stage for stories of unwavering resilience. Join us as we explore the theme of resilience, drawing inspiration from the courageous firefighters who navigate challenges with steadfast determination in the Centennial State.

Devotional: In the rugged terrain of Colorado, where nature's beauty meets its challenges, firefighters embody a resilience that echoes through the mountains and valleys. Whether facing wildfires, extreme weather, or other emergencies, their unwavering resolve reflects a reliance on a higher power and a commitment to protecting lives and landscapes. As we reflect on the resilience demonstrated by Colorado's firefighters, may we find strength in our faith and fortitude, trusting in the rock-solid foundation that sustains us through life's trials.

Reflection: Consider moments in your life when you faced challenges and found strength to overcome them. Reflect on the sources of resilience that have guided you through difficult times.

Prayer: Heavenly Father, we thank you for the resilience exhibited by the firefighters in Colorado. Bless them with continued strength and perseverance. May their example inspire us to find solace in you, our rock and fortress, as we navigate the challenges of life. Amen.

Action: In the spirit of resilience, tackle a challenge or obstacle that you have been putting off. Let this action be a testament to your inner strength and determination to overcome hurdles.

Week 7 - "Unity in Illinois"

Verse of the Week: "How good and pleasant it is when God's people live together in unity!" - Psalm 133:1 (NIV)

Introduction: This week, our devotional journey takes us to the heartland of America, to the state of Illinois, where the diverse landscapes and vibrant communities reflect a spirit of unity. Join us as we explore the theme of unity, drawing inspiration from the collaborative efforts of firefighters who work together to protect and serve in the Prairie State.

Devotional: In the mosaic of Illinois, where urban skylines meet vast farmlands, firefighters exemplify a spirit of unity that transcends differences. Whether responding to emergencies in bustling cities or rural areas, these heroes showcase the power of collaboration and togetherness. United by a common purpose, they serve their communities with strength drawn from a shared commitment to safety and well-being. As we reflect on the unity displayed by Illinois firefighters, may we find inspiration to foster harmony in our relationships and communities, recognizing the beauty that arises when people come together.

Reflection: Consider moments in your life when unity played a significant role. Reflect on the positive impact that collaboration and togetherness can have on achieving common goals.

Prayer: Gracious God, we thank you for the unity exhibited by the firefighters in Illinois. Bless them with continued collaboration and solidarity. May their example inspire us to seek harmony in our relationships, fostering a spirit of togetherness in our communities. Amen.

Action: In the spirit of unity, engage in an activity that promotes collaboration with others. Whether it's a community project, a team effort, or simply reaching out to connect with someone, let this action be a reflection of the strength found in unity.

Week 8 - "Dedication in Pennsylvania"

Verse of the Week: "Whatever you do, work at it with all your heart, as working for the Lord, not for human masters." - Colossians 3:23 (NIV)

Introduction: This week, our devotional journey takes us to the historic state of Pennsylvania, where the echoes of the past meet the vibrant energy of the present. Join us as we explore the theme of dedication, drawing inspiration from the committed firefighters who tirelessly serve the Keystone State with passion and purpose.

Devotional: In the heart of Pennsylvania, where history and innovation intertwine, firefighters exemplify a deep dedication that goes beyond duty. Whether preserving historic landmarks or responding to modern-day emergencies, these heroes approach their work with wholehearted commitment. Their dedication reflects not only a sense of responsibility to their communities but also a higher calling. As we reflect on the devotion displayed by Pennsylvania's firefighters, may we be inspired to approach our own endeavors with a similar sense of purpose, recognizing that true fulfillment comes from dedicating our efforts to something greater than ourselves.

Reflection: Consider moments in your life when dedication led to meaningful achievements. Reflect on the impact of committing wholeheartedly to your endeavors.

Prayer: Heavenly Father, we thank you for the dedication exhibited by the firefighters in Pennsylvania. Bless them with continued passion and purpose in their service. May their example inspire us to approach our work with diligence and a wholehearted commitment, recognizing that our efforts are ultimately for your glory. Amen.

Action: In the spirit of dedication, commit to a task or project with renewed passion this week. Let this action be a testament to the fulfillment that comes from giving your best effort to the things that matter most to you.

Week 9 - "Faithfulness in Georgia"

Verse of the Week: "Let love and faithfulness never leave you; bind them around your neck, write them on the tablet of your heart." - Proverbs 3:3 (NIV)

Introduction: This week, our devotional journey takes us to the warm and welcoming state of Georgia, where the southern charm meets a steadfast commitment to service. Join us as we explore the theme of faithfulness, drawing inspiration from the dedicated firefighters who exemplify unwavering loyalty to their communities in the Peach State.

Devotional: In the heart of Georgia, where hospitality and resilience converge, firefighters display a profound faithfulness in their service. Whether responding to emergencies or engaging in community outreach, these heroes demonstrate a commitment that endures through challenges. Their loyalty is not just a duty but a calling, reflecting a deep-rooted faithfulness to the well-being of those they serve. As we reflect on the faithfulness of Georgia's firefighters, may we be inspired to cultivate unwavering commitment in our own lives, binding love and faithfulness as guiding principles on the tablet of our hearts.

Reflection: Consider moments in your life when faithfulness played a significant role. Reflect on the impact of remaining steadfast in your commitments and relationships.

Prayer: Gracious God, we thank you for the faithfulness exhibited by the firefighters in Georgia. Bless them with continued loyalty and dedication. May their example inspire us to live with unwavering commitment, keeping love and faithfulness at the forefront of our hearts. Amen.

Action: In the spirit of faithfulness, commit to a small act of loyalty or service for someone in your life this week. Let this action be a reflection of your dedication to fostering meaningful connections and relationships.

Week 10 - "Perseverance in Arizona"

Verse of the Week: "Let us not become weary in doing good, for at the proper time we will reap a harvest if we do not give up." - Galatians 6:9 (NIV)

Introduction: This week, our devotional journey takes us to the captivating landscapes of Arizona, where the desert's beauty meets the resilience of those who call it home. Join us as we explore the theme of perseverance, drawing inspiration from the determined firefighters who face challenges head-on in the Grand Canyon State.

Devotional: In the vastness of Arizona, where the sunsets paint the sky with hues of red and orange, firefighters embody a spirit of perseverance that echoes through the canyons and deserts. Confronting wildfires, extreme temperatures, and various emergencies, these heroes stand firm in their commitment to protect lives and landscapes. Their perseverance is a testament to the belief that, even in the face of adversity, there is strength in endurance. As we reflect on the determination of Arizona's firefighters, may we find inspiration to persevere through our own challenges, trusting that, in due time, we will reap the rewards of our unwavering efforts.

Reflection: Consider moments in your life when perseverance led to positive outcomes. Reflect on the lessons learned through facing and overcoming challenges.

Prayer: Heavenly Father, we thank you for the perseverance exhibited by the firefighters in Arizona. Bless them with continued strength and endurance. May their example inspire us to face challenges with unwavering determination, knowing that your timing is perfect, and our efforts will bear fruit. Amen.

Action: In the spirit of perseverance, take a step toward overcoming a challenge or obstacle you've been facing. Let this action be a testament to your commitment to enduring through difficulties with faith and resilience.

Week 11 - "Gratitude in Tennessee"

Verse of the Week: "Give thanks in all circumstances; for this is God's will for you in Christ Jesus." - 1 Thessalonians 5:18 (NIV)

Introduction: This week, our devotional journey takes us to the scenic landscapes of Tennessee, where the rolling hills and music-filled air inspire a spirit of gratitude. Join us as we explore the theme of gratitude, drawing inspiration from the dedicated firefighters who express thankfulness for their communities in the Volunteer State.

Devotional: In the heart of Tennessee, where the sounds of country music resonate and the hospitality is as warm as the summer breeze, firefighters exemplify a profound sense of gratitude. Whether responding to emergencies or engaging in community outreach, these heroes express thankfulness for the opportunity to serve and protect. Their gratitude is a reflection of a deep appreciation for the communities they call home. As we reflect on the gratitude of Tennessee's firefighters, may we be inspired to cultivate a thankful heart, recognizing the blessings that surround us each day.

Reflection: Consider moments in your life when gratitude played a significant role. Reflect on the impact of expressing thankfulness and appreciation.

Prayer: Gracious God, we thank you for the gratitude exhibited by the firefighters in Tennessee. Bless them with continued appreciation for their communities. May their example inspire us to cultivate a thankful heart, expressing gratitude for the blessings in our lives. Amen.

Action: In the spirit of gratitude, take time each day this week to express thanks for something specific in your life. Whether big or small, let this action be a reflection of your appreciation for the blessings that surround you.

Week 12 - "Sacrifice in Massachusetts"

Verse of the Week: "Greater love has no one than this: to lay down one's life for one's friends." - John 15:13 (NIV)

Introduction: This week, our devotional journey takes us to the historic and culturally rich state of Massachusetts, where the legacy of sacrifice echoes through the cobblestone streets and revolutionary history. Join us as we explore the theme of sacrifice, drawing inspiration from the brave firefighters who embody selflessness in the Bay State.

Devotional: In the heart of Massachusetts, where history is etched into the landscapes and the spirit of sacrifice is honored, firefighters stand as symbols of selflessness. Whether rushing into burning buildings or facing other life-threatening situations, these heroes willingly sacrifice their safety for the well-being of others. Their actions mirror the profound love and sacrifice that transcend ordinary boundaries. As we reflect on the sacrifices made by Massachusetts' firefighters, may we find inspiration to cultivate a sacrificial spirit in our own lives, recognizing that love and selflessness are powerful agents of positive change.

Reflection: Consider moments in your life when sacrifices made a lasting impact. Reflect on the depth of love and selflessness that exists in your relationships and community.

Prayer: Heavenly Father, we thank you for the sacrifices exhibited by the firefighters in Massachusetts. Bless them with protection and courage. May their example inspire us to embrace sacrificial love, laying down our lives for the well-being of others. Amen.

Action: In the spirit of sacrifice, identify a way in which you can selflessly serve or support someone in need this week. Let this action be a reflection of your commitment to embodying sacrificial love in your daily life.

Week 13 - "Wisdom in Virginia"

Verse of the Week: "The fear of the Lord is the beginning of wisdom, and knowledge of the Holy One is understanding." - Proverbs 9:10 (NIV)

Introduction: This week, our devotional journey takes us to the historic and picturesque state of Virginia, where the echoes of the past blend with the wisdom of the present. Join us as we explore the theme of wisdom, drawing inspiration from the dedicated firefighters who exemplify discernment and understanding in the Old Dominion State.

Devotional: In the heart of Virginia, where history unfolds in every corner and the landscapes tell tales of wisdom, firefighters demonstrate a profound understanding in their service. Whether making split-second decisions during emergencies or imparting fire safety knowledge to communities, these heroes embody the essence of wisdom. Their discernment, coupled with practical knowledge, reflects a commitment to protecting lives and property. As we reflect on the wisdom displayed by Virginia's firefighters, may we be inspired to seek discernment and understanding in our own lives, recognizing that true wisdom begins with reverence for the source of all knowledge.

Reflection: Consider moments in your life when wisdom played a significant role. Reflect on the importance of seeking discernment and understanding in various aspects of your life.

Prayer: Gracious God, we thank you for the wisdom exhibited by the firefighters in Virginia. Bless them with continued discernment and understanding. May their example inspire us to seek wisdom, acknowledging that true understanding comes from reverence for you. Amen.

Action: In the spirit of wisdom, dedicate time this week to learn something new or seek guidance in a challenging situation. Let this action be a reflection of your commitment to cultivating discernment and understanding in your journey.

Week 14 - "Humility in Oregon"

Verse of the Week: "Do nothing out of selfish ambition or vain conceit. Rather, in humility value others above yourselves." - Philippians 2:3 (NIV)

Introduction: This week, our devotional journey takes us to the lush landscapes of Oregon, where nature's beauty is mirrored in the humble hearts of those who serve. Join us as we explore the theme of humility, drawing inspiration from the dedicated firefighters who exemplify selflessness and a servant's heart in the Beaver State.

Devotional: In the heart of Oregon, where towering forests and serene coastlines inspire awe, firefighters demonstrate a remarkable humility in their service. Whether facing the challenges of wildfire suppression or aiding communities in need, these heroes embody selflessness and a willingness to put the needs of others above their own. Their humility is a testament to the strength found in service to others. As we reflect on the humility displayed by Oregon's firefighters, may we be inspired to cultivate a humble heart in our own lives, recognizing the value of placing others above ourselves.

Reflection: Consider moments in your life when humility played a significant role. Reflect on the impact of selflessness and serving others with a humble heart.

Prayer: Heavenly Father, we thank you for the humility exhibited by the firefighters in Oregon. Bless them with continued selflessness and a servant's heart. May their example inspire us to value others above ourselves, embracing the strength found in humility. Amen.

Action: In the spirit of humility, actively seek opportunities to serve others without seeking recognition. Let this action be a reflection of your commitment to cultivating a humble and selfless heart in your daily interactions.

Week 15 - "Hope in Washington"

Verse of the Week: "May the God of hope fill you with all joy and peace as you trust in him, so that you may overflow with hope by the power of the Holy Spirit." - Romans 15:13 (NIV)

Introduction: This week, our devotional journey takes us to the evergreen landscapes of Washington, where the towering mountains and tranquil waters inspire a spirit of hope. Join us as we explore the theme of hope, drawing inspiration from the resilient firefighters who embody optimism and unwavering faith in the Evergreen State.

Devotional: In the heart of Washington, where the beauty of nature reflects a sense of renewal, firefighters display a remarkable hope in the face of challenges. Whether battling wildfires or responding to emergencies, these heroes exemplify optimism and an unwavering faith in the possibility of brighter days. Their hope is a beacon that guides them through adversity, illuminating a path for others to follow. As we reflect on the hope displayed by Washington's firefighters, may we be inspired to cultivate optimism and trust in the midst of our own trials, knowing that, through the power of hope, we can overcome even the darkest of circumstances.

Reflection: Consider moments in your life when hope played a significant role. Reflect on the impact of maintaining optimism and trust during challenging times.

Prayer: Gracious God, we thank you for the hope exhibited by the firefighters in Washington. Bless them with continued optimism and unwavering faith. May their example inspire us to trust in your promises, allowing hope to fill our hearts and guide us through every circumstance. Amen.

Action: In the spirit of hope, share words of encouragement or perform a random act of kindness for someone who may be going through a difficult time. Let this action be a reflection of the hope and positivity you wish to spread in the lives of others.

Week 16 - "Service in Maryland"

Verse of the Week: "For even the Son of Man did not come to be served, but to serve, and to give his life as a ransom for many." - Mark 10:45 (NIV)

Introduction: This week, our devotional journey takes us to the historically rich state of Maryland, where the legacy of service is woven into the fabric of its communities. Join us as we explore the theme of service, drawing inspiration from the dedicated firefighters who exemplify selfless acts of kindness and sacrifice in the Old Line State.

Devotional: In the heart of Maryland, where the echoes of history resound and communities thrive, firefighters embody a profound spirit of service. Whether responding to emergencies or engaging in community outreach, these heroes selflessly give of themselves to ensure the well-being of others. Their commitment to serving goes beyond duty; it is a calling that reflects the essence of love in action. As we reflect on the service displayed by Maryland's firefighters, may we be inspired to embrace opportunities for selfless acts, recognizing that true fulfillment is found in serving others with a compassionate heart.

Reflection: Consider moments in your life when acts of service brought joy and fulfillment. Reflect on the impact of selfless giving and kindness in your relationships and community.

Prayer: Heavenly Father, we thank you for the spirit of service exhibited by the firefighters in Maryland. Bless them with continued compassion and a heart for others. May their example inspire us to actively seek ways to serve, following the example of your Son, Jesus Christ. Amen.

Action: In the spirit of service, actively seek opportunities to help someone in need this week. Whether it's a small act of kindness or a larger gesture, let this action be a reflection of your commitment to selflessly serve others.

Week 17 - "Compassion in Louisiana"

Verse of the Week: "As God's chosen ones, holy and beloved, clothe yourselves with compassion, kindness, humility, meekness, and patience." - Colossians 3:12 (NRSV)

Introduction: This week, our devotional journey takes us to the vibrant and culturally rich state of Louisiana, where the rhythms of jazz and the warmth of hospitality set the stage for acts of compassion. Join us as we explore the theme of compassion, drawing inspiration from the dedicated firefighters who embody kindness and empathy in the Pelican State.

Devotional: In the heart of Louisiana, where the melody of compassion resonates through communities, firefighters exemplify a profound spirit of empathy. Whether responding to emergencies or engaging in outreach efforts, these heroes extend a helping hand with kindness and humility. Their compassion is a garment they wear daily, enveloping them in the understanding of others' struggles. As we reflect on the compassion displayed by Louisiana's firefighters, may we be inspired to clothe ourselves in kindness, embracing the call to love our neighbors as an expression of our faith.

Reflection: Consider moments in your life when acts of compassion made a lasting impact. Reflect on the importance of empathy and understanding in fostering connections with others.

Prayer: Gracious God, we thank you for the compassion exhibited by the firefighters in Louisiana. Bless them with continued kindness and empathy. May their example inspire us to clothe ourselves with compassion, extending love and understanding to those around us. Amen.

Action: In the spirit of compassion, intentionally reach out to someone who may be going through a challenging time. Offer a listening ear or a helping hand, allowing your actions to be a reflection of the compassionate love you wish to share.

Week 18 - "Courage in Alaska"

Verse of the Week: "Be strong and courageous. Do not be afraid or terrified because of them, for the Lord your God goes with you; he will never leave you nor forsake you." - Deuteronomy 31:6 (NIV)

Introduction: This week, our devotional journey takes us to the breathtaking landscapes of Alaska, where the vast wilderness and icy peaks reflect the resilience of those who call the Last Frontier home. Join us as we explore the theme of courage, drawing inspiration from the brave firefighters who navigate challenges in the face of adversity in the Great Land.

Devotional: In the heart of Alaska, where the rugged terrain and untamed beauty test the limits of bravery, firefighters stand as beacons of courage. Whether battling wildfires, enduring harsh conditions, or responding to emergencies, these heroes demonstrate an unparalleled strength that transcends the physical challenges they face. Their courage is rooted in a trust that God goes with them, providing unwavering support. As we reflect on the courage displayed by Alaska's firefighters, may we find inspiration to face our fears with the assurance that we are never alone in our journey.

Reflection: Consider moments in your life when courage played a significant role. Reflect on the challenges you faced and the strength that emerged when you trusted in a higher power.

Prayer: Heavenly Father, we thank you for the courage exhibited by the firefighters in Alaska. Bless them with continued strength and unwavering faith. May their example inspire us to be strong and courageous, trusting in your presence in every circumstance. Amen.

Action: In the spirit of courage, confront a fear or challenge that you've been hesitant to face. Let this action be a testament to your growing courage and trust in God's guidance.

Week 19 - "Unity in Hawaii"

Verse of the Week: "How good and pleasant it is when God's people live together in unity!" - Psalm 133:1 (NIV)

Introduction: This week, our devotional journey takes us to the tropical paradise of Hawaii, where the vibrant spirit of aloha and the serene beauty of the islands inspire a sense of unity. Join us as we explore the theme of unity, drawing inspiration from the dedicated firefighters who work collaboratively to protect the aloha spirit in the Rainbow State.

Devotional: In the heart of Hawaii, where the waves gently kiss the shores and the warmth of aloha fills the air, firefighters exemplify a unique unity that goes beyond the diverse landscapes of the islands. Whether responding to emergencies or engaging in community service, these heroes showcase the power of working together harmoniously. Their unity is a reflection of the interconnectedness that defines the aloha spirit, fostering a sense of 'ohana' (family) among all. As we reflect on the unity displayed by Hawaii's firefighters, may we be inspired to embrace the beauty of diversity and work collaboratively for the greater good.

Reflection: Consider moments in your life when unity brought about positive outcomes. Reflect on the impact of harmonious collaboration in your relationships and community.

Prayer: Gracious God, we thank you for the unity exhibited by the firefighters in Hawaii. Bless them with continued collaboration and 'ohana' spirit. May their example inspire us to live together in unity, recognizing the strength that comes from embracing diversity. Amen.

Action: In the spirit of unity, seek to build bridges with someone from a different background or perspective. Engage in a conversation to better understand and appreciate the diversity around you, fostering a sense of 'ohana' in your community.

Week 20 - "Resilience in Montana"

Verse of the Week: "I can do all things through Christ who strengthens me." - Philippians 4:13 (NKJV)

Introduction: This week, our devotional journey takes us to the vast and rugged landscapes of Montana, where the untamed wilderness and expansive horizons echo the resilience of those who call the Treasure State home. Join us as we explore the theme of resilience, drawing inspiration from the courageous firefighters who face challenges with unwavering determination in Big Sky Country.

Devotional: In the heart of Montana, where the mountains reach for the sky and the open plains stretch endlessly, firefighters embody a resilience that mirrors the unyielding spirit of the land. Confronting wildfires, extreme weather, and various emergencies, these heroes showcase a determination that is rooted in a source greater than themselves. Their resilience is a testament to the strength found in reliance on Christ. As we reflect on the resilience displayed by Montana's firefighters, may we find inspiration to face life's challenges with a steadfast spirit, trusting that through Christ, we can overcome any obstacle.

Reflection: Consider moments in your life when resilience played a significant role. Reflect on the strength you derived from your faith and determination.

Prayer: Heavenly Father, we thank you for the resilience exhibited by the firefighters in Montana. Bless them with continued determination and reliance on your strength. May their example inspire us to face challenges with unwavering faith, knowing that through Christ, we can conquer all things. Amen.

Action: In the spirit of resilience, tackle a challenge or obstacle this week with the assurance that Christ strengthens you. Let this action be a testament to your unwavering faith and determination in the face of adversity.

Week 21 - "Generosity in Vermont"

Verse of the Week: "Each of you should give what you have decided in your heart to give, not reluctantly or under compulsion, for God loves a cheerful giver." - 2 Corinthians 9:7 (NIV)

Introduction: This week, our devotional journey takes us to the picturesque landscapes of Vermont, where the rolling hills and vibrant seasons set the stage for acts of generosity. Join us as we explore the theme of generosity, drawing inspiration from the dedicated firefighters who selflessly give of themselves to serve the Green Mountain State.

Devotional: In the heart of Vermont, where nature's beauty reflects a simplicity of life, firefighters demonstrate a remarkable generosity that extends beyond their duty. Whether responding to emergencies or supporting community initiatives, these heroes embody the spirit of cheerful giving. Their generosity is not compelled by duty but driven by a genuine desire to uplift and support others. As we reflect on the generosity displayed by Vermont's firefighters, may we be inspired to give selflessly, recognizing that true fulfillment comes from a heart that overflows with generosity.

Reflection: Consider moments in your life when acts of generosity brought joy and fulfillment. Reflect on the impact of giving with a cheerful heart.

Prayer: Gracious God, we thank you for the generosity exhibited by the firefighters in Vermont. Bless them with continued cheerful hearts and abundance. May their example inspire us to give selflessly, recognizing the joy that comes from uplifting and supporting others. Amen.

Action: In the spirit of generosity, find a way to give to someone in need this week. Whether it's your time, resources, or a simple act of kindness, let this action be a reflection of your commitment to cheerful giving.

Week 22 - "Endurance in Utah"

Verse of the Week: "Therefore, since we are surrounded by such a great cloud of witnesses, let us throw off everything that hinders and the sin that so easily entangles. And let us run with perseverance the race marked out for us." - Hebrews 12:1 (NIV)

Introduction: This week, our devotional journey takes us to the rugged and majestic landscapes of Utah, where the towering red rocks and expansive deserts symbolize the endurance needed to navigate life's challenges. Join us as we explore the theme of endurance, drawing inspiration from the dedicated firefighters who display resilience and perseverance in the Beehive State.

Devotional: In the heart of Utah, where the landscapes speak of both beauty and challenges, firefighters embody an enduring spirit in their service. Confronting wildfires, extreme conditions, and various emergencies, these heroes persevere with determination and resilience. Their endurance is a testament to the strength found in running the race marked out for them. As we reflect on the endurance displayed by Utah's firefighters, may we find inspiration to throw off hindrances and run our own race with perseverance, knowing that we are surrounded by a great cloud of witnesses.

Reflection: Consider moments in your life when endurance played a significant role. Reflect on the challenges you faced and the perseverance that emerged in overcoming obstacles.

Prayer: Heavenly Father, we thank you for the endurance exhibited by the firefighters in Utah. Bless them with continued resilience and perseverance. May their example inspire us to run our race with determination, throwing off hindrances and trusting in your strength. Amen.

Action: In the spirit of endurance, identify a challenge or obstacle you've been facing, and take a step toward overcoming it this week. Let this action be a reflection of your commitment to persevering in the race marked out for you.

Week 23 - "Hope in New Mexico"

Verse of the Week: "Now faith is confidence in what we hope for and assurance about what we do not see." - Hebrews 11:1 (NIV)

Introduction: This week, our devotional journey takes us to the enchanting landscapes of New Mexico, where the vibrant culture and vast deserts inspire a sense of hope. Join us as we explore the theme of hope, drawing inspiration from the dedicated firefighters who bring reassurance and optimism to the Land of Enchantment.

Devotional: In the heart of New Mexico, where the colors of the desert paint a canvas of beauty, firefighters embody a resilient hope in their service. Facing wildfires, unpredictable conditions, and various emergencies, these heroes carry a confidence in their commitment to protecting lives and landscapes. Their hope is rooted in faith, an assurance that transcends the visible challenges they confront. As we reflect on the hope displayed by New Mexico's firefighters, may we find inspiration to cultivate a hopeful spirit in our own lives, placing confidence in the promises that extend beyond what we can see.

Reflection: Consider moments in your life when hope played a significant role. Reflect on the impact of maintaining optimism and trust during challenging times.

Prayer: Gracious God, we thank you for the hope exhibited by the firefighters in New Mexico. Bless them with continued optimism and unwavering faith. May their example inspire us to embrace hope, trusting in your promises even in the face of uncertainty. Amen.

Action: In the spirit of hope, encourage someone who may be going through a difficult time this week. Share words of assurance and optimism, allowing your actions to be a reflection of the hope you carry in your heart.

Week 24 - "Peace in Maine"

Verse of the Week: "Peace I leave with you; my peace I give you. I do not give to you as the world gives. Do not let your hearts be troubled and do not be afraid." - John 14:27 (NIV)

Introduction: This week, our devotional journey takes us to the serene landscapes of Maine, where the rugged coastlines and tranquil forests inspire a sense of peace. Join us as we explore the theme of peace, drawing inspiration from the dedicated firefighters who bring calmness and reassurance to the Pine Tree State.

Devotional: In the heart of Maine, where the soothing sounds of nature provide a backdrop to daily life, firefighters embody a profound peace in their service. Whether responding to emergencies or providing assistance in the community, these heroes carry a calmness that transcends the chaos they may face. Their peace is rooted in the assurance of their calling and the desire to bring tranquility to those they serve. As we reflect on the peace displayed by Maine's firefighters, may we find inspiration to cultivate a sense of calm in our own lives, trusting in the peace that surpasses understanding.

Reflection: Consider moments in your life when peace played a significant role. Reflect on the impact of maintaining calmness and reassurance in the midst of challenges.

Prayer: Heavenly Father, we thank you for the peace exhibited by the firefighters in Maine. Bless them with continued calmness and assurance. May their example inspire us to embrace peace, trusting in your promises and finding tranquility even in the midst of life's storms. Amen.

Action: In the spirit of peace, take intentional moments of stillness and quiet reflection this week. Allow these moments to bring calmness to your heart and mind, trusting in the peace that comes from God's presence.

Week 25 - "Service in Michigan"

Verse of the Week: "For even the Son of Man did not come to be served, but to serve, and to give his life as a ransom for many." - Mark 10:45 (NIV)

Introduction: This week, our devotional journey takes us to the heart of the Great Lakes in Michigan, where the expansive waters and diverse landscapes symbolize the spirit of service. Join us as we explore the theme of service, drawing inspiration from the dedicated firefighters who selflessly give of themselves to protect and serve the Great Lakes State.

Devotional: In the heart of Michigan, where the waters connect communities and the landscapes vary from bustling cities to serene forests, firefighters exemplify a profound spirit of service. Whether responding to emergencies or engaging in community outreach, these heroes selflessly give of their time and efforts to ensure the well-being of others. Their commitment to serving goes beyond duty; it is a calling that reflects the essence of love in action. As we reflect on the service displayed by Michigan's firefighters, may we be inspired to actively seek ways to serve, following the example of Jesus who came not to be served, but to serve.

Reflection: Consider moments in your life when acts of service brought joy and fulfillment. Reflect on the impact of selfless giving and kindness in your relationships and community.

Prayer: Heavenly Father, we thank you for the spirit of service exhibited by the firefighters in Michigan. Bless them with continued compassion and a heart for others. May their example inspire us to actively seek ways to serve, following the example of your Son, Jesus Christ. Amen.

Action: In the spirit of service, actively seek opportunities to help someone in need this week. Whether it's a small act of kindness or a larger gesture, let this action be a reflection of your commitment to selflessly serve others.

Week 26 - "Gratitude in Kentucky"

Verse of the Week: "Give thanks to the Lord, for he is good; his love endures forever." - 1 Chronicles 16:34 (NIV)

Introduction: This week, our devotional journey takes us to the bluegrass fields and rolling hills of Kentucky, where the spirit of hospitality and the echoes of history inspire a sense of gratitude. Join us as we explore the theme of gratitude, drawing inspiration from the dedicated firefighters who express thankfulness for their communities in the Bluegrass State.

Devotional: In the heart of Kentucky, where the sound of bluegrass music fills the air and the hospitality is as warm as the sunlit fields, firefighters exemplify a profound sense of gratitude. Whether responding to emergencies or engaging in community outreach, these heroes express thankfulness for the opportunity to serve and protect. Their gratitude is a reflection of a deep appreciation for the communities they call home. As we reflect on the gratitude of Kentucky's firefighters, may we be inspired to cultivate a thankful heart, recognizing the blessings that surround us each day.

Reflection: Consider moments in your life when gratitude played a significant role. Reflect on the impact of expressing thankfulness and appreciation.

Prayer: Gracious God, we thank you for the gratitude exhibited by the firefighters in Kentucky. Bless them with continued appreciation for their communities. May their example inspire us to cultivate a thankful heart, expressing gratitude for the blessings in our lives. Amen.

Action: In the spirit of gratitude, take time each day this week to express thanks for something specific in your life. Whether big or small, let this action be a reflection of your appreciation for the blessings that surround you.

Week 27 - "Compassion in Connecticut"

Verse of the Week: "As God's chosen ones, holy and beloved, clothe yourselves with compassion, kindness, humility, meekness, and patience." - Colossians 3:12 (NRSV)

Introduction: This week, our devotional journey takes us to the picturesque landscapes and historic communities of Connecticut, where the spirit of compassion flows through the quaint towns and bustling cities. Join us as we explore the theme of compassion, drawing inspiration from the dedicated firefighters who embody kindness and empathy in the Constitution State.

Devotional: In the heart of Connecticut, where colonial architecture meets modern living, firefighters exemplify a profound spirit of compassion. Whether responding to emergencies or engaging in community outreach, these heroes extend a helping hand with kindness and humility. Their compassion is a garment they wear daily, enveloping them in the understanding of others' struggles. As we reflect on the compassion displayed by Connecticut's firefighters, may we be inspired to clothe ourselves with kindness, embracing the call to love our neighbors as an expression of our faith.

Reflection: Consider moments in your life when acts of compassion made a lasting impact. Reflect on the importance of empathy and understanding in fostering connections with others.

Prayer: Gracious God, we thank you for the compassion exhibited by the firefighters in Connecticut. Bless them with continued kindness and empathy. May their example inspire us to clothe ourselves with compassion, extending love and understanding to those around us. Amen.

Action: In the spirit of compassion, intentionally reach out to someone who may be going through a challenging time. Offer a listening ear or a helping hand, allowing your actions to be a reflection of the compassionate love you wish to share.

Week 28 - "Hope in Ohio"

Verse of the Week: "May the God of hope fill you with all joy and peace as you trust in him, so that you may overflow with hope by the power of the Holy Spirit." - Romans 15:13 (NIV)

Introduction: This week, our devotional journey takes us to the heart of the Midwest, to the welcoming state of Ohio, where the landscapes are as diverse as the communities that thrive within them. Join us as we explore the theme of hope, drawing inspiration from the dedicated firefighters who bring optimism and resilience to the Buckeye State.

Devotional: In the heart of Ohio, where fields of green meet bustling cityscapes, firefighters embody a remarkable hope in their service. Whether responding to emergencies, aiding in community outreach, or supporting one another, these heroes showcase an unwavering faith in the possibility of brighter days. Their hope is a beacon that guides them through adversity, illuminating a path for others to follow. As we reflect on the hope displayed by Ohio's firefighters, may we be inspired to cultivate optimism and trust in the midst of our own trials, knowing that, through the power of hope, we can overcome even the darkest of circumstances.

Reflection: Consider moments in your life when hope played a significant role. Reflect on the impact of maintaining optimism and trust during challenging times.

Prayer: Gracious God, we thank you for the hope exhibited by the firefighters in Ohio. Bless them with continued optimism and unwavering faith. May their example inspire us to trust in your promises, allowing hope to fill our hearts and guide us through every circumstance. Amen.

Action: In the spirit of hope, share words of encouragement or perform a random act of kindness for someone who may be going through a difficult time. Let this action be a reflection of the hope and positivity you wish to spread in the lives of others.

Week 29 - "Courage in Nevada"

Verse of the Week: "Be strong and courageous. Do not be afraid or terrified because of them, for the Lord your God goes with you; he will never leave you nor forsake you." - Deuteronomy 31:6 (NIV)

Introduction: This week, our devotional journey takes us to the expansive landscapes of Nevada, where the vast deserts and vibrant cities symbolize the courage needed to face life's challenges. Join us as we explore the theme of courage, drawing inspiration from the dedicated firefighters who navigate difficulties with unwavering strength in the Silver State.

Devotional: In the heart of Nevada, where the desert sunsets paint the skies with hues of orange and pink, firefighters embody a courageous spirit in their service. Whether battling wildfires, responding to emergencies, or aiding communities in need, these heroes face challenges with determination and resilience. Their courage is rooted in the assurance that God goes with them, providing unwavering support. As we reflect on the courage displayed by Nevada's firefighters, may we find inspiration to confront our fears with the knowledge that we are never alone in our journey.

Reflection: Consider moments in your life when courage played a significant role. Reflect on the challenges you faced and the strength that emerged when you trusted in a higher power.

Prayer: Heavenly Father, we thank you for the courage exhibited by the firefighters in Nevada. Bless them with continued strength and unwavering faith. May their example inspire us to be strong and courageous, trusting in your presence in every circumstance. Amen.

Action: In the spirit of courage, confront a fear or challenge that you've been hesitant to face. Let this action be a testament to your growing courage and trust in God's guidance.

Week 30 - "Resilience in Idaho"

Verse of the Week: "I can do all things through Christ who strengthens me." - Philippians 4:13 (NKJV)

Introduction: This week, our devotional journey takes us to the rugged and diverse landscapes of Idaho, where the majestic mountains and vast wilderness symbolize the resilience needed to endure life's challenges. Join us as we explore the theme of resilience, drawing inspiration from the dedicated firefighters who face adversity with unwavering determination in the Gem State.

Devotional: In the heart of Idaho, where the landscapes vary from rolling hills to towering peaks, firefighters embody a resilience that mirrors the unyielding spirit of the land. Confronting wildfires, extreme weather, and various emergencies, these heroes showcase a determination that is rooted in a source greater than themselves. Their resilience is a testament to the strength found in reliance on Christ. As we reflect on the resilience displayed by Idaho's firefighters, may we find inspiration to face life's challenges with a steadfast spirit, trusting that through Christ, we can overcome any obstacle.

Reflection: Consider moments in your life when resilience played a significant role. Reflect on the strength you derived from your faith and determination.

Prayer: Heavenly Father, we thank you for the resilience exhibited by the firefighters in Idaho. Bless them with continued determination and reliance on your strength. May their example inspire us to face challenges with unwavering faith, knowing that through Christ, we can conquer all things. Amen.

Action: In the spirit of resilience, tackle a challenge or obstacle this week with the assurance that Christ strengthens you. Let this action be a testament to your unwavering faith and determination in the face of adversity.

Week 31 - "Stewardship in Wyoming"

Verse of the Week: "The earth is the Lord's, and everything in it, the world, and all who live in it." - Psalm 24:1 (NIV)

Introduction: This week, our devotional journey takes us to the wide-open spaces and majestic landscapes of Wyoming, where the untamed wilderness and rugged beauty inspire a sense of stewardship for the Creator's creation. Join us as we explore the theme of stewardship, drawing inspiration from the dedicated firefighters who serve as stewards of the land in the Equality State.

Devotional: In the heart of Wyoming, where the mountains touch the sky and the prairies stretch endlessly, firefighters embody a profound sense of stewardship for the natural beauty that surrounds them. Whether combating wildfires, preserving wildlife habitats, or responding to environmental emergencies, these heroes recognize the responsibility to care for the earth. Their actions reflect an understanding that the land is a gift from the Lord, and they are entrusted with its protection. As we reflect on the stewardship displayed by Wyoming's firefighters, may we be inspired to cultivate a sense of responsibility for the environment, recognizing our role as stewards of God's creation.

Reflection: Consider moments in your life when you've been called to be a steward of the environment. Reflect on the impact of responsible actions in caring for the earth.

Prayer: Gracious God, we thank you for the stewardship exhibited by the firefighters in Wyoming. Bless them with continued wisdom and diligence in caring for the land. May their example inspire us to be responsible stewards of the environment, recognizing the beauty and significance of your creation. Amen.

Action: In the spirit of stewardship, engage in an environmentally friendly activity or initiative this week. Whether it's recycling, participating in a cleanup, or supporting conservation efforts, let this action be a reflection of your commitment to caring for God's creation.

Week 32 - "Community in North Dakota"

Verse of the Week: "Two are better than one, because they have a good return for their labor: If either of them falls down, one can help the other up." - Ecclesiastes 4:9-10 (NIV)

Introduction: This week, our devotional journey takes us to the serene landscapes and tight-knit communities of North Dakota, where the vast plains and strong sense of community inspire a commitment to mutual support. Join us as we explore the theme of community, drawing inspiration from the dedicated firefighters who exemplify the power of togetherness in the Peace Garden State.

Devotional: In the heart of North Dakota, where the fields stretch to the horizon and small communities thrive, firefighters embody a profound sense of community. Whether responding to emergencies, engaging in outreach, or supporting one another, these heroes showcase the strength that emerges when individuals come together for a common purpose. Their unity is a reflection of the biblical truth that two are better than one, and together they can overcome challenges. As we reflect on the community spirit displayed by North Dakota's firefighters, may we be inspired to strengthen our bonds with others, recognizing the significance of mutual support in our lives.

Reflection: Consider moments in your life when the support of a community made a positive impact. Reflect on the strength found in coming together with others.

Prayer: Heavenly Father, we thank you for the sense of community exhibited by the firefighters in North Dakota. Bless them with continued unity and mutual support. May their example inspire us to foster strong connections within our communities, recognizing the power of togetherness. Amen.

Action: In the spirit of community, reach out to someone in your community this week. Whether it's a neighbor, friend, or coworker, offer a helping hand or a word of encouragement, fostering a sense of togetherness in your surroundings.

Week 33 - "Gratitude in South Dakota"

Verse of the Week: "Give thanks to the Lord, for he is good; his love endures forever." - Psalm 107:1 (NIV)

Introduction: This week, our devotional journey takes us to the vast landscapes and rich history of South Dakota, where the open prairies and iconic landmarks inspire a profound sense of gratitude. Join us as we explore the theme of gratitude, drawing inspiration from the dedicated firefighters who express thankfulness for their communities in the Mount Rushmore State.

Devotional: In the heart of South Dakota, where the sunsets paint the skies with vibrant colors and the land tells stories of the past, firefighters embody a remarkable spirit of gratitude. Whether responding to emergencies or engaging in community outreach, these heroes express thankfulness for the opportunity to serve and protect. Their gratitude is a reflection of a deep appreciation for the communities they call home. As we reflect on the gratitude of South Dakota's firefighters, may we be inspired to cultivate a thankful heart, recognizing the blessings that surround us each day.

Reflection: Consider moments in your life when gratitude played a significant role. Reflect on the impact of expressing thankfulness and appreciation.

Prayer: Gracious God, we thank you for the gratitude exhibited by the firefighters in South Dakota. Bless them with continued appreciation for their communities. May their example inspire us to cultivate a thankful heart, expressing gratitude for the blessings in our lives. Amen.

Action: In the spirit of gratitude, take time each day this week to express thanks for something specific in your life. Whether big or small, let this action be a reflection of your appreciation for the blessings that surround you.

Week 34 - "Generosity in Nebraska"

Verse of the Week: "A generous person will prosper; whoever refreshes others will be refreshed." - Proverbs 11:25 (NIV)

Introduction: This week, our devotional journey takes us to the expansive plains and warm communities of Nebraska, where the spirit of generosity and hospitality flows like the meandering rivers. Join us as we explore the theme of generosity, drawing inspiration from the dedicated firefighters who embody a selfless giving of themselves in the Cornhusker State.

Devotional: In the heart of Nebraska, where the fields stretch to the horizon and communities come together, firefighters exemplify a remarkable spirit of generosity. Whether responding to emergencies, aiding those in need, or supporting community initiatives, these heroes showcase a selfless giving that goes beyond duty. Their generosity is a reflection of the biblical truth that a generous person will prosper, not only materially but also in the richness of spirit. As we reflect on the generosity displayed by Nebraska's firefighters, may we be inspired to cultivate a spirit of giving, refreshing others as we ourselves are refreshed.

Reflection: Consider moments in your life when acts of generosity brought joy and fulfillment. Reflect on the impact of selfless giving in your relationships and community.

Prayer: Heavenly Father, we thank you for the generosity exhibited by the firefighters in Nebraska. Bless them with continued abundance and a heart for others. May their example inspire us to be generous, refreshing others with acts of kindness and love. Amen.

Action: In the spirit of generosity, actively seek opportunities to help someone in need this week. Whether it's a small act of kindness or a larger gesture, let this action be a reflection of your commitment to selflessly serve and refresh others.

Week 35 - "Unity in Kansas"

Verse of the Week: "How good and pleasant it is when God's people live together in unity!" - Psalm 133:1 (NIV)

Introduction: This week, our devotional journey takes us to the heart of the Midwest, to the expansive plains and warm communities of Kansas. Join us as we explore the theme of unity, drawing inspiration from the dedicated firefighters who work collaboratively to protect and serve the Sunflower State.

Devotional: In the heart of Kansas, where the golden fields stretch as far as the eye can see and communities thrive, firefighters exemplify a unique unity that transcends differences. Whether responding to emergencies in small towns or large cities, these heroes showcase the power of working together harmoniously. Their unity is a reflection of the strength that emerges when diverse individuals come together for a common purpose. As we reflect on the unity displayed by Kansas's firefighters, may we be inspired to celebrate diversity, recognizing the beauty and strength that arise when God's people live together in unity.

Reflection: Consider moments in your life when unity brought about positive outcomes. Reflect on the impact of harmonious collaboration in your relationships and community.

Prayer: Gracious God, we thank you for the unity exhibited by the firefighters in Kansas. Bless them with continued collaboration and a spirit of togetherness. May their example inspire us to live together in unity, celebrating the diversity that reflects your creative design. Amen.

Action: In the spirit of unity, seek to build bridges with someone from a different background or perspective. Engage in a conversation to better understand and appreciate the diversity around you, fostering a sense of togetherness in your community.

Week 36 - "Strength in Oklahoma"

Verse of the Week: "The Lord is my strength and my shield; my heart trusts in him, and he helps me. My heart leaps for joy, and with my song I praise him." - Psalm 28:7 (NIV)

Introduction: This week, our devotional journey takes us to the diverse landscapes and resilient communities of Oklahoma, where the plains, hills, and cities symbolize the strength needed to face life's challenges. Join us as we explore the theme of strength, drawing inspiration from the dedicated firefighters who embody resilience and fortitude in the Sooner State.

Devotional: In the heart of Oklahoma, where the winds sweep across the plains and communities rise against adversity, firefighters exemplify a profound strength in their service. Whether battling wildfires, responding to emergencies, or aiding communities in need, these heroes face challenges with determination and resilience. Their strength is rooted in the trust they place in the Lord, who is their shield and source of help. As we reflect on the strength displayed by Oklahoma's firefighters, may we find inspiration to trust in the Lord for our strength, allowing our hearts to leap for joy in the face of challenges.

Reflection: Consider moments in your life when strength played a significant role. Reflect on the challenges you faced and the trust you placed in the Lord for help.

Prayer: Heavenly Father, we thank you for the strength exhibited by the firefighters in Oklahoma. Bless them with continued determination and unwavering faith. May their example inspire us to find our strength in you, trusting in your help and finding joy in your presence. Amen.

Action: In the spirit of strength, face a challenge this week with the assurance that the Lord is your strength and shield. Let this action be a testament to your trust in God's guidance and a source of joy in your heart.

Week 37 - "Compassion in Minnesota"

Verse of the Week: "As God's chosen ones, holy and beloved, clothe yourselves with compassion, kindness, humility, meekness, and patience." - Colossians 3:12 (NRSV)

Introduction: This week, our devotional journey takes us to the land of lakes and forests, to the welcoming communities of Minnesota. Join us as we explore the theme of compassion, drawing inspiration from the dedicated firefighters who embody kindness and empathy in the North Star State.

Devotional: In the heart of Minnesota, where the lakes glisten and the communities thrive, firefighters exemplify a profound spirit of compassion. Whether responding to emergencies or engaging in community outreach, these heroes extend a helping hand with kindness and humility. Their compassion is a garment they wear daily, enveloping them in the understanding of others' struggles. As we reflect on the compassion displayed by Minnesota's firefighters, may we be inspired to clothe ourselves with kindness, embracing the call to love our neighbors as an expression of our faith.

Reflection: Consider moments in your life when acts of compassion made a lasting impact. Reflect on the importance of empathy and understanding in fostering connections with others.

Prayer: Gracious God, we thank you for the compassion exhibited by the firefighters in Minnesota. Bless them with continued kindness and empathy. May their example inspire us to clothe ourselves with compassion, extending love and understanding to those around us. Amen.

Action: In the spirit of compassion, intentionally reach out to someone who may be going through a challenging time. Offer a listening ear or a helping hand, allowing your actions to be a reflection of the compassionate love you wish to share.

Week 38 - "Community in Iowa"

Verse of the Week: "How good and pleasant it is when God's people live together in unity!" - Psalm 133:1 (NIV)

Introduction: This week, our devotional journey takes us to the heart of the Midwest, to the picturesque landscapes and tight-knit communities of Iowa. Join us as we explore the theme of community, drawing inspiration from the dedicated firefighters who exemplify the power of togetherness in the Hawkeye State.

Devotional: In the heart of Iowa, where the fields stretch to the horizon and communities are tightly woven, firefighters embody a profound sense of community. Whether responding to emergencies, engaging in outreach, or supporting one another, these heroes showcase the strength that emerges when individuals come together for a common purpose. Their unity is a reflection of the biblical truth that how good and pleasant it is when God's people live together in unity. As we reflect on the community spirit displayed by Iowa's firefighters, may we be inspired to strengthen our bonds with others, recognizing the significance of mutual support in our lives.

Reflection: Consider moments in your life when the support of a community made a positive impact. Reflect on the strength found in coming together with others.

Prayer: Heavenly Father, we thank you for the sense of community exhibited by the firefighters in Iowa. Bless them with continued unity and mutual support. May their example inspire us to foster strong connections within our communities, recognizing the power of togetherness. Amen.

Action: In the spirit of community, reach out to someone in your community this week. Whether it's a neighbor, friend, or coworker, offer a helping hand or a word of encouragement, fostering a sense of togetherness in your surroundings.

Week 39 - "Resilience in Missouri"

Verse of the Week: "I can do all things through him who strengthens me." - Philippians 4:13 (ESV)

Introduction: This week, our devotional journey takes us to the heart of the Midwest, to the diverse landscapes and resilient communities of Missouri. Join us as we explore the theme of resilience, drawing inspiration from the dedicated firefighters who embody a steadfast spirit in the Show-Me State.

Devotional: In the heart of Missouri, where the rolling hills meet the mighty rivers, firefighters exemplify a remarkable resilience that mirrors the unyielding spirit of the land. Confronting various challenges, responding to emergencies, and supporting communities in need, these heroes showcase a determination rooted in a source greater than themselves. Their resilience is a testament to the strength found in reliance on God. As we reflect on the resilience displayed by Missouri's firefighters, may we find inspiration to face life's challenges with a steadfast spirit, trusting that through Him who strengthens us, we can overcome any obstacle.

Reflection: Consider moments in your life when resilience played a significant role. Reflect on the strength you derived from your faith and determination.

Prayer: Heavenly Father, we thank you for the resilience exhibited by the firefighters in Missouri. Bless them with continued determination and reliance on your strength. May their example inspire us to face challenges with unwavering faith, knowing that through Christ, we can conquer all things. Amen.

Action: In the spirit of resilience, tackle a challenge or obstacle this week with the assurance that Christ strengthens you. Let this action be a testament to your unwavering faith and determination in the face of adversity.

Week 40 - "Courage in Arkansas"

Verse of the Week: "Be strong and courageous. Do not be afraid; do not be discouraged, for the Lord your God will be with you wherever you go." - Joshua 1:9 (NIV)

Introduction: This week, our devotional journey takes us to the natural beauty and warm communities of Arkansas, where the hills, rivers, and vibrant cities inspire a profound sense of courage. Join us as we explore the theme of courage, drawing inspiration from the dedicated firefighters who navigate challenges with unwavering strength in the Natural State.

Devotional: In the heart of Arkansas, where the landscapes are as diverse as the communities that thrive within them, firefighters embody a courageous spirit in their service. Whether responding to emergencies, aiding communities in need, or facing the unpredictable forces of nature, these heroes display determination and resilience. Their courage is grounded in the assurance that God goes with them, providing unwavering support. As we reflect on the courage displayed by Arkansas's firefighters, may we find inspiration to confront our fears with the knowledge that we are never alone in our journey.

Reflection: Consider moments in your life when courage played a significant role. Reflect on the challenges you faced and the strength that emerged when you trusted in a higher power.

Prayer: Heavenly Father, we thank you for the courage exhibited by the firefighters in Arkansas. Bless them with continued strength and unwavering faith. May their example inspire us to be strong and courageous, trusting in your presence in every circumstance. Amen.

Action: In the spirit of courage, confront a fear or challenge that you've been hesitant to face. Let this action be a testament to your growing courage and trust in God's guidance.

Week 41 - "Compassion in Wisconsin"

Verse of the Week: "And be kind and compassionate to one another, forgiving one another, just as God also forgave you in Christ." - Ephesians 4:32 (CSB)

Introduction: This week, our devotional journey takes us to the picturesque landscapes and welcoming communities of Wisconsin, where the lakeshores, forests, and vibrant cities inspire a profound sense of compassion. Join us as we explore the theme of compassion, drawing inspiration from the dedicated firefighters who embody kindness and empathy in the Badger State.

Devotional: In the heart of Wisconsin, where the seasons change and communities thrive, firefighters exemplify a remarkable spirit of compassion. Whether responding to emergencies, engaging in community outreach, or supporting one another, these heroes extend a helping hand with kindness and humility. Their compassion is a reflection of the biblical call to be kind and compassionate, forgiving one another. As we reflect on the compassion displayed by Wisconsin's firefighters, may we be inspired to extend grace to those around us, recognizing the transformative power of compassion and forgiveness.

Reflection: Consider moments in your life when acts of compassion and forgiveness made a lasting impact. Reflect on the importance of empathy and understanding in fostering connections with others.

Prayer: Gracious God, we thank you for the compassion exhibited by the firefighters in Wisconsin. Bless them with continued kindness and empathy. May their example inspire us to be compassionate and forgiving, reflecting the love and grace you have shown us in Christ. Amen.

Action: In the spirit of compassion, intentionally extend kindness to someone this week. Whether through a word of encouragement, a thoughtful gesture, or an act of forgiveness, let this action be a reflection of the compassionate love you wish to share with others.

Week 42 - "Unity in Indiana"

Verse of the Week: "How good and pleasant it is when God's people live together in unity!" - Psalm 133:1 (NIV)

Introduction: This week, our devotional journey takes us to the heart of the Midwest, to the diverse landscapes and thriving communities of Indiana. Join us as we explore the theme of unity, drawing inspiration from the dedicated firefighters who work collaboratively to protect and serve the Hoosier State.

Devotional: In the heart of Indiana, where small towns and bustling cities coexist, firefighters exemplify a unique unity that transcends differences. Whether responding to emergencies in rural areas or urban centers, these heroes showcase the power of working together harmoniously. Their unity is a reflection of the strength that emerges when diverse individuals come together for a common purpose. As we reflect on the unity displayed by Indiana's firefighters, may we be inspired to celebrate diversity, recognizing the beauty and strength that arise when God's people live together in unity.

Reflection: Consider moments in your life when unity brought about positive outcomes. Reflect on the impact of harmonious collaboration in your relationships and community.

Prayer: Gracious God, we thank you for the unity exhibited by the firefighters in Indiana. Bless them with continued collaboration and a spirit of togetherness. May their example inspire us to live together in unity, celebrating the diversity that reflects your creative design. Amen.

Action: In the spirit of unity, seek to build bridges with someone from a different background or perspective. Engage in a conversation to better understand and appreciate the diversity around you, fostering a sense of togetherness in your community.

Week 43 - "Hope in West Virginia"

Verse of the Week: "May the God of hope fill you with all joy and peace as you trust in him, so that you may overflow with hope by the power of the Holy Spirit." - Romans 15:13 (NIV)

Introduction: This week, our devotional journey takes us to the beautiful landscapes and resilient communities of West Virginia, where the mountains and valleys inspire a profound sense of hope. Join us as we explore the theme of hope, drawing inspiration from the dedicated firefighters who bring optimism and resilience to the Mountain State.

Devotional: In the heart of West Virginia, where the hills and rivers create a tapestry of natural beauty, firefighters embody a remarkable hope in their service. Whether responding to emergencies, aiding in community outreach, or supporting one another, these heroes showcase an unwavering faith in the possibility of brighter days. Their hope is a beacon that guides them through adversity, illuminating a path for others to follow. As we reflect on the hope displayed by West Virginia's firefighters, may we be inspired to cultivate optimism and trust in the midst of our own trials, knowing that, through the power of hope, we can overcome even the darkest of circumstances.

Reflection: Consider moments in your life when hope played a significant role. Reflect on the impact of maintaining optimism and trust during challenging times.

Prayer: Gracious God, we thank you for the hope exhibited by the firefighters in West Virginia. Bless them with continued optimism and unwavering faith. May their example inspire us to trust in your promises, allowing hope to fill our hearts and guide us through every circumstance. Amen.

Action: In the spirit of hope, share words of encouragement or perform a random act of kindness for someone who may be going through a difficult time. Let this action be a reflection of the hope and positivity you wish to spread in the lives of others.

Week 44 - "Courage in Mississippi"

Verse of the Week: "Be strong and courageous. Do not be afraid or terrified because of them, for the Lord your God goes with you; he will never leave you nor forsake you." - Deuteronomy 31:6 (NIV)

Introduction: This week, our devotional journey takes us to the warm landscapes and resilient communities of Mississippi, where the river flows and the magnolias bloom, inspiring a profound sense of courage. Join us as we explore the theme of courage, drawing inspiration from the dedicated firefighters who navigate challenges with unwavering strength in the Magnolia State.

Devotional: In the heart of Mississippi, where the rich history and diverse communities come together, firefighters exemplify a courageous spirit in their service. Whether responding to emergencies, aiding communities in need, or facing the unpredictable forces of nature, these heroes showcase determination and resilience. Their courage is grounded in the assurance that God goes with them, providing unwavering support. As we reflect on the courage displayed by Mississippi's firefighters, may we find inspiration to confront our fears with the knowledge that we are never alone in our journey.

Reflection: Consider moments in your life when courage played a significant role. Reflect on the challenges you faced and the strength that emerged when you trusted in a higher power.

Prayer: Heavenly Father, we thank you for the courage exhibited by the firefighters in Mississippi. Bless them with continued strength and unwavering faith. May their example inspire us to be strong and courageous, trusting in your presence in every circumstance. Amen.

Action: In the spirit of courage, confront a fear or challenge that you've been hesitant to face. Let this action be a testament to your growing courage and trust in God's guidance.

Week 45 - "Faith in Alabama"

Verse of the Week: "Now faith is the assurance of things hoped for, the conviction of things not seen." - Hebrews 11:1 (ESV)

Introduction: This week, our devotional journey takes us to the heart of the Deep South, to the vibrant landscapes and resilient communities of Alabama, where the sweet magnolias bloom, and the spirit of faith thrives. Join us as we explore the theme of faith, drawing inspiration from the dedicated firefighters who embody unwavering trust in the Heart of Dixie.

Devotional: In the heart of Alabama, where history and hospitality intertwine, firefighters exemplify a remarkable faith in their service. Whether responding to emergencies, aiding communities in need, or facing the unknown challenges of each day, these heroes showcase a profound trust in the unseen. Their faith is grounded in the assurance that their efforts make a difference and that they are part of a greater purpose. As we reflect on the faith displayed by Alabama's firefighters, may we find inspiration to cultivate our own faith, trusting in the assurance of things hoped for, even when they are not seen.

Reflection: Consider moments in your life when faith played a significant role. Reflect on the impact of trusting in the unseen and the assurance it brings.

Prayer: Gracious God, we thank you for the faith exhibited by the firefighters in Alabama. Bless them with continued assurance and unwavering trust. May their example inspire us to cultivate a deep and abiding faith, trusting in your guidance and purpose for our lives. Amen.

Action: In the spirit of faith, take a step of trust this week in an area of your life where you may be uncertain. Let this action be a testament to your growing faith and reliance on the unseen guidance of a higher power.

Week 46 - "Unity in South Carolina"

Verse of the Week: "How good and pleasant it is when God's people live together in unity!" - Psalm 133:1 (NIV)

Introduction: This week, our devotional journey takes us to the warm landscapes and close-knit communities of South Carolina, where the palmetto trees sway and the spirit of unity thrives. Join us as we explore the theme of unity, drawing inspiration from the dedicated firefighters who work collaboratively to protect and serve the Palmetto State.

Devotional: In the heart of South Carolina, where history and hospitality intersect, firefighters exemplify a unique unity that transcends differences. Whether responding to emergencies in bustling cities or rural areas, these heroes showcase the power of working together harmoniously. Their unity is a reflection of the strength that emerges when diverse individuals come together for a common purpose. As we reflect on the unity displayed by South Carolina's firefighters, may we be inspired to celebrate diversity, recognizing the beauty and strength that arise when God's people live together in unity.

Reflection: Consider moments in your life when unity brought about positive outcomes. Reflect on the impact of harmonious collaboration in your relationships and community.

Prayer: Gracious God, we thank you for the unity exhibited by the firefighters in South Carolina. Bless them with continued collaboration and a spirit of togetherness. May their example inspire us to live together in unity, celebrating the diversity that reflects your creative design. Amen.

Action: In the spirit of unity, seek to build bridges with someone from a different background or perspective. Engage in a conversation to better understand and appreciate the diversity around you, fostering a sense of togetherness in your community.

Week 47 - "Gratitude in North Dakota"

Verse of the Week: "Give thanks to the Lord, for he is good; his love endures forever." - Psalm 107:1 (NIV)

Introduction: This week, our devotional journey takes us to the vast landscapes and tight-knit communities of North Dakota, where the plains stretch far and the spirit of gratitude thrives. Join us as we explore the theme of gratitude, drawing inspiration from the dedicated firefighters who express thankfulness for their communities in the Peace Garden State.

Devotional: In the heart of North Dakota, where the winds blow across the open prairies and communities thrive, firefighters embody a profound spirit of gratitude. Whether responding to emergencies or engaging in community outreach, these heroes express thankfulness for the opportunity to serve and protect. Their gratitude is a reflection of the deep appreciation they hold for the communities they call home. As we reflect on the gratitude displayed by North Dakota's firefighters, may we be inspired to cultivate a thankful heart, recognizing the blessings that surround us each day.

Reflection: Consider moments in your life when gratitude played a significant role. Reflect on the impact of expressing thankfulness and appreciation.

Prayer: Gracious God, we thank you for the gratitude exhibited by the firefighters in North Dakota. Bless them with continued appreciation for their communities. May their example inspire us to cultivate a thankful heart, expressing gratitude for the blessings in our lives. Amen.

Action: In the spirit of gratitude, take time each day this week to express thanks for something specific in your life. Whether big or small, let this action be a reflection of your appreciation for the blessings that surround you.

Week 48 - "Community in Delaware"

Verse of the Week: "How good and pleasant it is when God's people live together in unity!" - Psalm 133:1 (NIV)

Introduction: This week, our devotional journey takes us to the charming landscapes and close-knit communities of Delaware, where the coastal beauty meets historical richness, inspiring a profound sense of community. Join us as we explore the theme of community, drawing inspiration from the dedicated firefighters who exemplify the power of togetherness in the First State.

Devotional: In the heart of Delaware, where the rivers flow and the communities thrive, firefighters embody a profound sense of community. Whether responding to emergencies, engaging in outreach, or supporting one another, these heroes showcase the strength that emerges when individuals come together for a common purpose. Their unity is a reflection of the biblical truth that how good and pleasant it is when God's people live together in unity. As we reflect on the community spirit displayed by Delaware's firefighters, may we be inspired to strengthen our bonds with others, recognizing the significance of mutual support in our lives.

Reflection: Consider moments in your life when the support of a community made a positive impact. Reflect on the strength found in coming together with others.

Prayer: Heavenly Father, we thank you for the sense of community exhibited by the firefighters in Delaware. Bless them with continued unity and mutual support. May their example inspire us to foster strong connections within our communities, recognizing the power of togetherness. Amen.

Action: In the spirit of community, reach out to someone in your community this week. Whether it's a neighbor, friend, or coworker, offer a helping hand or a word of encouragement, fostering a sense of togetherness in your surroundings.

Week 49 - "Resilience in New Jersey"

Verse of the Week: "I can do all things through him who strengthens me." - Philippians 4:13 (ESV)

Introduction: This week, our devotional journey takes us to the diverse landscapes and resilient communities of New Jersey, where the shorelines meet bustling cities, inspiring a profound sense of resilience. Join us as we explore the theme of resilience, drawing inspiration from the dedicated firefighters who embody determination and fortitude in the Garden State.

Devotional: In the heart of New Jersey, where the cities thrive and the communities stand strong, firefighters exemplify a remarkable resilience in their service. Whether responding to emergencies, aiding communities in need, or facing unforeseen challenges, these heroes showcase a determination rooted in the belief that they can do all things through Him who strengthens them. As we reflect on the resilience displayed by New Jersey's firefighters, may we find inspiration to face life's challenges with unwavering faith and the assurance that, with God's strength, we can overcome any obstacle.

Reflection: Consider moments in your life when resilience played a significant role. Reflect on the strength you derived from your faith and determination.

Prayer: Heavenly Father, we thank you for the resilience exhibited by the firefighters in New Jersey. Bless them with continued determination and unwavering faith. May their example inspire us to face challenges with a steadfast spirit, trusting in your strength and guidance. Amen.

Action: In the spirit of resilience, tackle a challenge or obstacle this week with the assurance that the Lord is your strength. Let this action be a testament to your trust in God's guidance and a source of joy in your heart.

Week 50 - "Hope in Rhode Island"

Verse of the Week: "Now faith is confidence in what we hope for and assurance about what we do not see." - Hebrews 11:1 (NIV)

Introduction: This week, our devotional journey takes us to the serene landscapes and close-knit communities of Rhode Island, where the ocean meets charming towns, inspiring a profound sense of hope. Join us as we explore the theme of hope, drawing inspiration from the dedicated firefighters who bring optimism and resilience to the Ocean State.

Devotional: In the heart of Rhode Island, where the waves gently kiss the shoreline and communities stand resilient, firefighters exemplify a remarkable hope in their service. Whether responding to emergencies, aiding in community outreach, or supporting one another, these heroes showcase an unwavering faith in the possibility of brighter days. Their hope is a beacon that guides them through adversity, illuminating a path for others to follow. As we reflect on the hope displayed by Rhode Island's firefighters, may we be inspired to cultivate optimism and trust in the midst of our own trials, knowing that through the power of hope, we can overcome even the darkest of circumstances.

Reflection: Consider moments in your life when hope played a significant role. Reflect on the impact of maintaining optimism and trust during challenging times.

Prayer: Gracious God, we thank you for the hope exhibited by the firefighters in Rhode Island. Bless them with continued optimism and unwavering faith. May their example inspire us to trust in your promises, allowing hope to fill our hearts and guide us through every circumstance. Amen.

Action: In the spirit of hope, share words of encouragement or perform a random act of kindness for someone who may be going through a difficult time. Let this action be a reflection of the hope and positivity you wish to spread in the lives of others.

Week 51 - "Community in New Hampshire"

Verse of the Week: "How good and pleasant it is when God's people live together in unity!" - Psalm 133:1 (NIV)

Introduction: This week, our devotional journey takes us to the picturesque landscapes and tight-knit communities of New Hampshire, where the mountains stand tall and the spirit of community thrives. Join us as we explore the theme of community, drawing inspiration from the dedicated firefighters who exemplify the power of togetherness in the Granite State.

Devotional: In the heart of New Hampshire, where the mountains whisper tales of resilience and the communities come together, firefighters embody a profound sense of community. Whether responding to emergencies, engaging in outreach, or supporting one another, these heroes showcase the strength that emerges when individuals come together for a common purpose. Their unity is a reflection of the biblical truth that how good and pleasant it is when God's people live together in unity. As we reflect on the community spirit displayed by New Hampshire's firefighters, may we be inspired to strengthen our bonds with others, recognizing the significance of mutual support in our lives.

Reflection: Consider moments in your life when the support of a community made a positive impact. Reflect on the strength found in coming together with others.

Prayer: Heavenly Father, we thank you for the sense of community exhibited by the firefighters in New Hampshire. Bless them with continued unity and mutual support. May their example inspire us to foster strong connections within our communities, recognizing the power of togetherness. Amen.

Action: In the spirit of community, reach out to someone in your community this week. Whether it's a neighbor, friend, or coworker, offer a helping hand or a word of encouragement, fostering a sense of togetherness in your surroundings.

Week 52 - "Unity in Washington, D.C."

Verse of the Week: "How good and pleasant it is when God's people live together in unity!" - Psalm 133:1 (NIV)

Introduction: This week, our devotional journey takes us to the heart of the nation, Washington, D.C., where history is etched in every monument and the spirit of unity resonates. Join us as we explore the theme of unity, drawing inspiration from the dedicated firefighters who work collaboratively to protect and serve the residents and visitors of the nation's capital.

Devotional: In Washington, D.C., where the iconic landmarks stand as symbols of freedom and democracy, firefighters exemplify a unique unity that transcends differences. Whether responding to emergencies in the heart of the city or providing assistance during national events, these heroes showcase the power of working together harmoniously. Their unity is a reflection of the strength that emerges when diverse individuals come together for a common purpose. As we reflect on the unity displayed by Washington, D.C.'s firefighters, may we be inspired to celebrate diversity, recognizing the beauty and strength that arise when God's people live together in unity.

Reflection: Consider moments in your life when unity brought about positive outcomes. Reflect on the impact of harmonious collaboration in your relationships and community.

Prayer: Gracious God, we thank you for the unity exhibited by the firefighters in Washington, D.C. Bless them with continued collaboration and a spirit of togetherness. May their example inspire us to live together in unity, celebrating the diversity that reflects your creative design. Amen.

Action: In the spirit of unity, seek to build bridges with someone from a different background or perspective. Engage in a conversation to better understand and appreciate the diversity around you, fostering a sense of togetherness in your community.

About the Author

Alan Bohms is not only an accomplished author but a dedicated servant of his community, serving as a volunteer firefighter with the McDonald Volunteer Fire Department in Mohawk, TN. With a commitment to ensuring the safety and well-being of others, Alan's journey extends beyond the pages of this devotional.

In addition to his role as a volunteer firefighter, Alan Bohms serves as the Executive Director of the Volunteer Firefighter Alliance, a national non-profit organization. Through his leadership, the alliance strives to support and uplift volunteer firefighters across the country, recognizing their invaluable contributions to communities large and small.

Alan brings a unique perspective to "In the Line of Faith: A 50-State Firefighter Devotional," drawing inspiration from his firsthand experiences on the front lines of service. His passion for celebrating the courage, resilience, and faith of firefighters shines through in the pages of this devotional, making it a heartfelt tribute to the unsung heroes who stand ready to answer the call.

Made in the USA
Columbia, SC
20 February 2025

2491aed4-2c33-4e10-a1b8-e30a48756aa1R01